HOW MAN BECAME

MARGERY MORRIS

Illustrations by
Michael Spink

Penguin Books

Contents

Early Primates	4
Ramapithecus	12
Australopithecines	19
Homo Erectus	27
Neanderthal Man	34
Homo Sapiens	38
Time and Change	46
Index	48

This book is for DIANA CAROLINE SANSOME

Penguin Books Ltd, Harmondsworth, Middlesex, England
Penguin Books Inc., 7110 Ambassador Road, Baltimore, Maryland 21207, U.S.A.
Penguin Books Australia Ltd, Ringwood, Victoria, Australia

First published 1972

Copyright © Margery Morris 1972

Illustrations and artwork copyright © Michael Spink and Penguin Education, 1972

Diagrams copyright © Penguin Education Ltd, 1972

Printed in Great Britain by Alabaster Passmore & Sons Ltd, Tovil, Maidstone, Kent

This book is sold subject to the condition that it shall not, by way of trade or otherwise, be lent, re-sold, hired out, or otherwise circulated without the publisher's prior consent in any form of binding or cover other than that in which it is published and without a similar condition including this condition being imposed on the subsequent purchaser

Quizkid, explorer in time, having investigated the life and death of dinosaurs,* has started to wonder about the origins of man. With the help of his 'geologic timepiece' he can travel through time, and once more he dials himself back through the ages to begin his new investigation.

* see *About Dinosaurs*

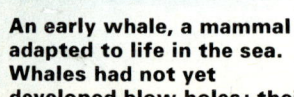

Early Primates

The Eocene – 54 Million Years Ago

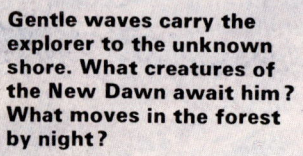

Gentle waves carry the explorer to the unknown shore. What creatures of the New Dawn await him? What moves in the forest by night?

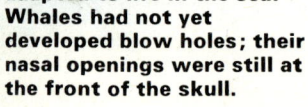

On such a raft as this many a creature must have drifted to distant shores. Quizkid's fellow traveller is an ancient tree shrew.

An early whale, a mammal adapted to life in the sea. Whales had not yet developed blow holes; their nasal openings were still at the front of the skull.

Birds are related to dinosaurs; they have an ancestor in common. It will be a long time before they learn to fear man.

Here a fallen tyrant laid his bones 70 million years ago or more.

This placid turtle is a reptile that did not die out. She lays her eggs in the sand.

Quizkid's best viewpoint is a handy tree. Man's ancestors, the early primates, lived in trees and only came out at night. This is a kind of tarsier. Look at his eyes, his hands, and his feet.

Adapis is a kind of lemur. Its baby is rocked to sleep in the treetops. If the bough breaks, a flying leap takes the mother to safety.

Diatryma is a flightless Eocene bird, 2·13 metres (7 feet) tall.

Hyaenodon is an early carnivore (flesh eater). He hopes a bough will break.

Little *Eohippus*, the Dawn Horse, is no bigger than a fox terrier. He browses on leaves, for there are no grasslands yet.

Snakes are successful reptiles who have adapted and survived.

This mammal is a fly-by-night.

Uintatherium **is not built for speed. His bony horns are too heavy and his brain is too small. He will not survive.**

Coryphodon **is an amblypod. He is an early herbivore (plant eater), despite those teeth. He ambles.**

Early Primates

When dinosaurs were dead and gone the mammals came out of hiding, to take possession of the earth and all its dwelling places.

By the Eocene (EE-o-seen), 10 million years after the death of the last dinosaur, all the main kinds of mammals had appeared, though they did not look very much like the mammals we know today.

There were herbivores, which ate plants, and carnivores, which ate meat, and omnivores, which ate anything they could get.

Mammalian Design

Mammals are 'warm-blooded'. Their temperature stays the same whatever the weather, so they are less at the mercy of the climate. They have more efficient breathing arrangements than the dinosaurs, for they can eat and breathe at the same time, and they have better circulation of the blood.

Babies of mammals grow inside the mother, and when they are born she nurses, protects and teaches them.

Mammals grow only two sets of teeth. (Dinosaur teeth were replaced whenever they dropped out.)

Mammals have fur or hair to keep the heat in, and sweat glands or pores to help them cool off.

Mammals are active, adaptable, and inquisitive.

Life in the Trees

In dinosaur days some little mammals took to the trees to escape the monsters. They were the first primates (PRY-mates).

Scientists divide all living things into different groups. The names of the main groups are: Kingdom, Phylum, Class, Order, Family, Genus, Species.

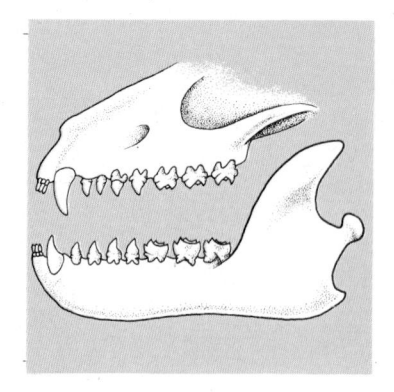

Ancient mammalian teeth. In each jaw are 3 *incisor* teeth, a sharp *canine* tooth, 4 *premolar* teeth, and 3 *molar* teeth. How many have you?

The primate order belongs to the *Class Mammalia* (Mam-AY-lia), the mammals, which in turn belong to the *Phylum Chordata* (FILE-um Cor-DAY-ta), the back-boned animals, which belong to the *Animal* (not the Vegetable or Mineral) *Kingdom*.

The primate order includes man himself, and all his relations, the living and fossil apes, monkeys, lemurs, tarsiers, and tree shrews.

In the world of the tree dweller paths are narrow and swaying, the light greenish and changeable. The earth far below is hard, and the carnivores are waiting. If a bough cracks, tree dwellers must jump, reach, grip. They won't get a second chance.

So, in time, the early primates gradually developed or evolved:

(a) *hands and feet* (and sometimes tails) which could grasp well. Fingers and toes had nails, not claws, in most of them.

(b) *eyes* with stereoscopic vision. Each eye gives a separate picture. With stereoscopic vision the brain combines the two: you see things in depth (3-D), not flat like a photograph, so they are easier to recognize. Primates also evolved colour vision.

(c) *brains* enlarged to take messages from the senses, sort them out, and translate them quickly into action.

Tree Shrew

Tarsier

Monkey

Human

Primate grips: From claws to human grip, with fully opposable thumb.

vision smell

Tree Shrew   Monkey   Man

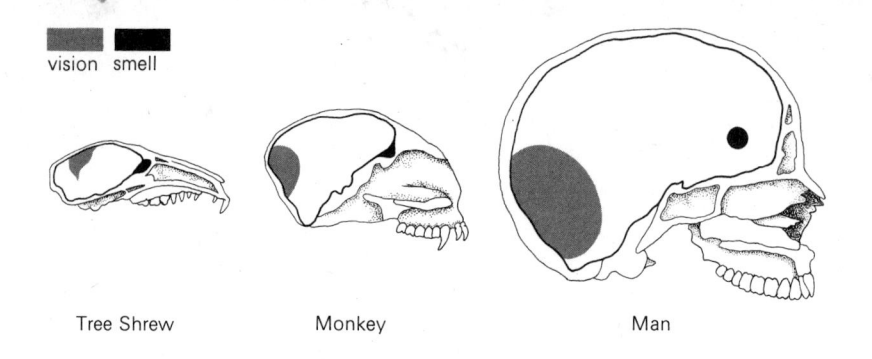

Primates didn't need their sense of smell so much in the trees, and the old 'smell brain' got smaller.

The brains of mammals had always been better than dinosaur brains. Now primate brains grew larger.

Primate noses got shorter, faces became flatter, and the eyes came forward, one on each side of the nose.

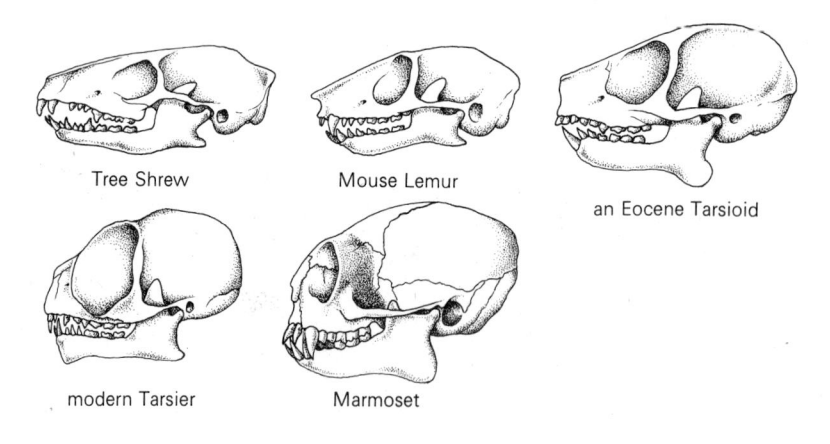

Tree Shrew   Mouse Lemur   an Eocene Tarsioid

modern Tarsier   Marmoset

Brain cases got bigger, and muzzles got flatter.

Primate mothers usually have only one baby at a time. (Imagine trying to look after a whole litter in a tree top.)

The primates didn't *choose* to change in these ways. But the animals who gradually developed the most useful changes were the ones who survived and had more babies like themselves.

How Evolution Works

When a male and a female mate, the sperm and the egg come together to make a cell which will grow into a baby.

Inside the parents' sperm and egg cells are genes — tiny units which 'programme' the growth of the new individual. The baby inherits genes from both parents, and these genes exactly duplicate themselves in the new baby, making it look like its parents and relations.

Sometimes the genes inherited by the baby are not exactly like those of the parents. One or more of them will have quite suddenly changed, or *mutated*. The mutation may help the baby to adapt better to its environment, and the same mutated gene will go on duplicating itself when the baby eventually has babies of its own.

The white cub didn't decide to have white fur. It had white fur because it inherited a mutated gene. In a snowy climate it will have a better chance of surviving. This is called Natural Selection.

The primates in the trees were selected by Nature for the things that made it easier for them to survive — their hands and feet, their eyes, and their brains.

In a brownish landscape the brown cub is not easy to spot, as it is well adapted to its surroundings. The white cub has inherited a mutated gene and is not so lucky. The eagle is about to seize the conspicuous white cub.

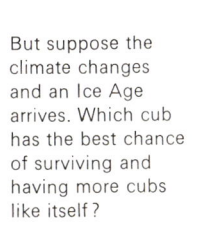

But suppose the climate changes and an Ice Age arrives. Which cub has the best chance of surviving and having more cubs like itself?

11

Ramapithecus

The Miocene – 26 million years ago

The world is changing; the forests are shrinking, and broad grasslands take their place.

A very old carnivore waits hopefully in the water.
Learning to walk on your hind legs is very difficult.

Mischievous juveniles have found new games to play. Quizkid strives to keep his temper. 'Bi-pedal hominids! Most interesting, very active. STOP IT!'

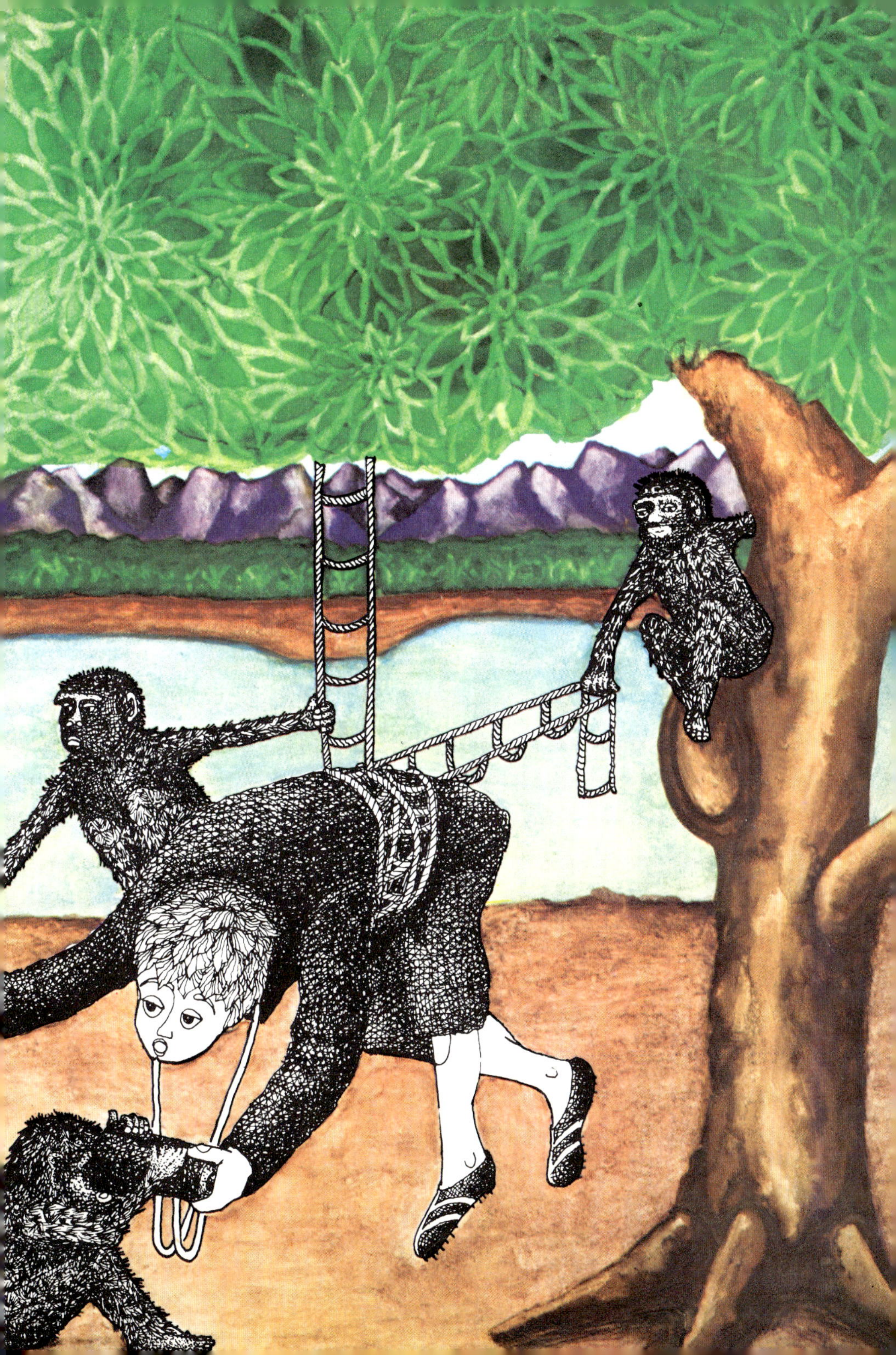

Miocene monkeys live mostly in the trees. Not for them the perilous open spaces.

Other mammals have left the forest for the plains. Giant hogs root for tubers.

What kind of ape is this, using his forelimbs to carry food and a weapon?

The old lady's back seems to hurt her. Is walking upright a strain on her spine?

Ramapithecus

Time and change together did their silent work over the slow millions of years. The 16 million years of the Eocene were followed by the 12 million years of the Oligocene (OLLY-go-seen).

By the Oligocene new kinds of primates had evolved from some of the little tarsioids. Their bones have been found in Europe, North America, and in Egypt.

Primate remains are hard to find. They lived in forests, and forest floors don't form the sort of rocks in which fossils are preserved.

But in Egypt, for instance, rivers flowed through the tropical jungle. Dead animals fell into the river and were entombed in the mud which gradually formed into rock to be found by explorers 40 million years later.

The new primates were little creatures, not quite monkeys, not quite apes. Among them was *Aegyptopithecus* (Ee-JIP-toc pith EEK-us). His fossil remains have been found not only in Egypt but in East Africa. He is an exciting discovery, because he may have been the long-sought ancestor of both apes and man.

The Oligocene was followed by the Miocene (MY-o-seen), which lasted for 19 million years. By Miocene times there were many apes, large and small, and they seem to have inhabited all the forests of the world. They flourished particularly in Central Africa. *Proconsul* was one of them.

One primate of the Late Miocene was different. He lived in Kenya and in India. Sooner or later his fossil bones may be found in other places too. He was a primate who moved around.

The Kenya primate was called *Kenyapithecus* (Ken-ya-pith-EEK-us) by his discoverer. His Indian relation was *Ramapithecus* (Rah-ma-pith-EEK-us), and this is what most scientists call him now. Almost the only thing known

Proconsul was a Miocene ape who probably spent a lot of time on the ground.

about *Ramapithecus* is his teeth, so when we find more of him our picture will change. But his teeth are extremely interesting.

Most primates have large sharp canine teeth and use them to attack or to defend themselves.

But *Ramapithecus* had small canines. Was he an exceptionally peaceable animal? Possibly. But it was more likely that he used his hands to defend himself. Battered lumps of lava and smashed bones and antelope skulls were found with the Kenya fossils, showing that *Ramapithecus* may have used crude tools to obtain bone marrow and brains.

And if he used his hands, then he must have walked on his hind legs some, or even most, of the time. How did this great evolutionary change come about?

Towards the end of the Miocene the world grew dryer and the forests retreated. Grassy plains appeared. Some four-footed mammals like the elephant, and the hog, and the horse, and the giraffe, and the antelope took to the grasslands.

Some primates stayed in the trees, but *Ramapithecus* came down to the ground. Primates are adventurous. They like to explore open ground.

So we can guess (though we can't prove any of it yet) that *Ramapithecus* lived on the plains, walking on his hind legs. His hands were free to bring food quite long distances to share with his family. He could brandish sticks at the animals who attacked him, or throw things at them. He could use stones to bash things, and sticks to dig for roots and tubers.

Ramapithecus children couldn't use their feet to grip their mother's fur like monkeys.

Probably they had to be carried. So perhaps the females and juveniles were left behind, while the males hunted.

No doubt *Ramapithecus* could still climb trees if he wanted to. Perhaps he slept in them.

Ramapithecus was not only a primate, he was a *Hominid*.

The primate order has two sub-orders, the *Prosimii* (Pro-SIMMY-i) and the *Anthropoidea* (An-thro-POID-eea). The *Prosimii* includes the tree shrews, lemurs, lorises and tarsiers, living and extinct. The

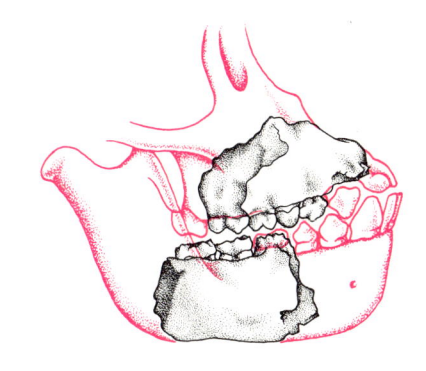

The jaws and face region of *Ramapithecus*.

Anthropoidea is divided into three superfamilies: the Ceboidea (See-BOID-eea) – the American monkeys; the Cercopithecoidea (Cerco-pithy-COID-eea) – the other monkeys; and the Hominoidea (hom-in-OID-eea). The Hominoidea, meaning 'man-like creatures', is sub-divided into two families – the *Pongidae* (Pon-GID-ee), the apes, living and extinct, and the *Hominidae* (Ho-MIN-i-dee), men, living and extinct.

So we have
        Class: Mammalia
        Order: Primates
        Suborder: Anthropoidea
        Suborder: Prosimii
        Superfamily: Ceboidea
        Superfamily: Cercopithecoidea
        Superfamily: Hominoidea
        Family: Pongidae
        Family: Hominidae

Ramapithecus was a member of the *Hominidae*, man's family. We were his future.

This baboon shows his teeth when he feels angry. What threatening gesture does man make when he's getting ready to fight?

Australopithecines

The Pleistocene – 2·1 million years ago

On the shores of an ancient lake in Africa australopithecine hominids lived.
For a startled moment past and future are reflected side by side.

Australopithecines were probably small-time hunters, but the baboon is isolated and they hope to catch it by stealth and cunning, fierce as it is.

Was it a sabre-tooth tiger, a baboon, a crocodile, that gave him this dreadful wound?

A zebra's rib bone smoothes the hide. The skin will make a bed, or a cover, or a sling to carry the baby in.

Tempers seem to run high. Perhaps everyone is a little hungry or tired for they have no fire to keep the predators away at night.

Bones can be opened to get at the marrow – an enjoyable occupation.

The toolmaker whistles contentedly, the morning sun warm on his back. The quartz and lava to make these pebble tools came from a distance.

Australopithecines

From the late Miocene to the early Pleistocene (PLY-sto-seen) and the australopithecines is a great leap in time. The 5 million years of the Pliocene (PLY-o-seen) lie between. During the Pliocene the upright ape must have evolved and perfected his walking, and improved upon his hunting. But the fossils which tell us how he changed and became more manlike are still waiting to be found. They will probably be found in Africa – man's early home.

The Southern Apes

In 1925 the bones of early Pleistocene hominids were found in South Africa.

The hominid was given the name *Australopithecus* (Aw-stra-lo-pith-EEK-us), 'the Southern Ape'. But the australopithecines were not apes. They had small canine teeth, and their hip bones, limbs and jaws were almost like man's. Their brains were about half the size of modern man's. Later their remains were found in other parts of Africa.

There were two kinds: *Australopithecus robustus*, who was bigger and heavier, and probably a vegetarian. He died out about 500,000 years ago. It was *Australopithecus africanus*, the second kind, who seems to have been the ancestor of modern man.

The very earliest remains of australopithecines so far discovered are about 4 million years old. They were found in Ethiopia.

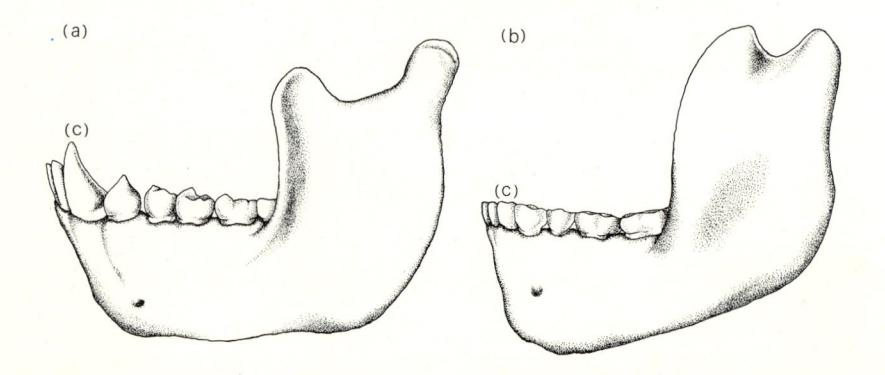

(a) The lower jaw of a modern ape. (b) The jaw of an australopithecine. Note the canines (c).

Olduvai Gorge

Olduvai Gorge in Tanzania is the best place in the world to see where and how early man lived. Here, 1,750,000 years ago, australopithecines dwelt on the shores of a lake. Volcanoes simmered on the horizon. Many other animals shared the plains with them, strange short-necked giraffes with antlers, enormous elephants with tusks in their lower jaws, sabre-toothed tigers, jackals, hyenas, bat-eared foxes, and little three-toed horses.

How did the hominids survive? We know they ate small game like frogs, lizards, hares, and ducks because the bones are there on their *living floor*. (Modern palaeontologists do not just dig; they take pains to uncover the living floor – the whole area where the ancient hominids lived and worked – so that we can understand more about the way they arranged their lives.)

Probably the australopithecines were wily hunters. They certainly tackled baboons. Possibly they scavenged. The plains then, as now, must have been littered with the bodies and whitening bones of predators' victims.

Tools were found at Olduvai too. (Some palaeontologists think that these tools were made by a third kind of man, *Homo habilis* – 'the man with ability'.) But whoever made them, these tools were *shaped*; they were not just lumps of rock. The most common tool was a chopper made out of a pebble. Until recently the Olduvai pebble tools were the oldest known. But now tools have been found at East Rudolf in Kenya which are 800,000 years older.

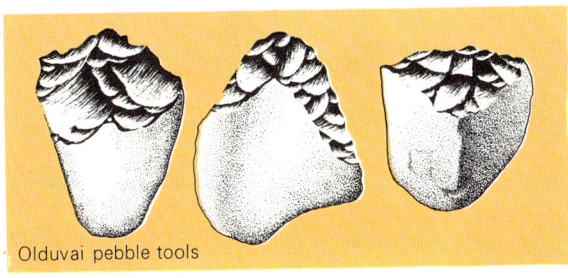

Libytherium, an antlered giraffe from the early Pleistocene in Africa.

Olduvai pebble tools

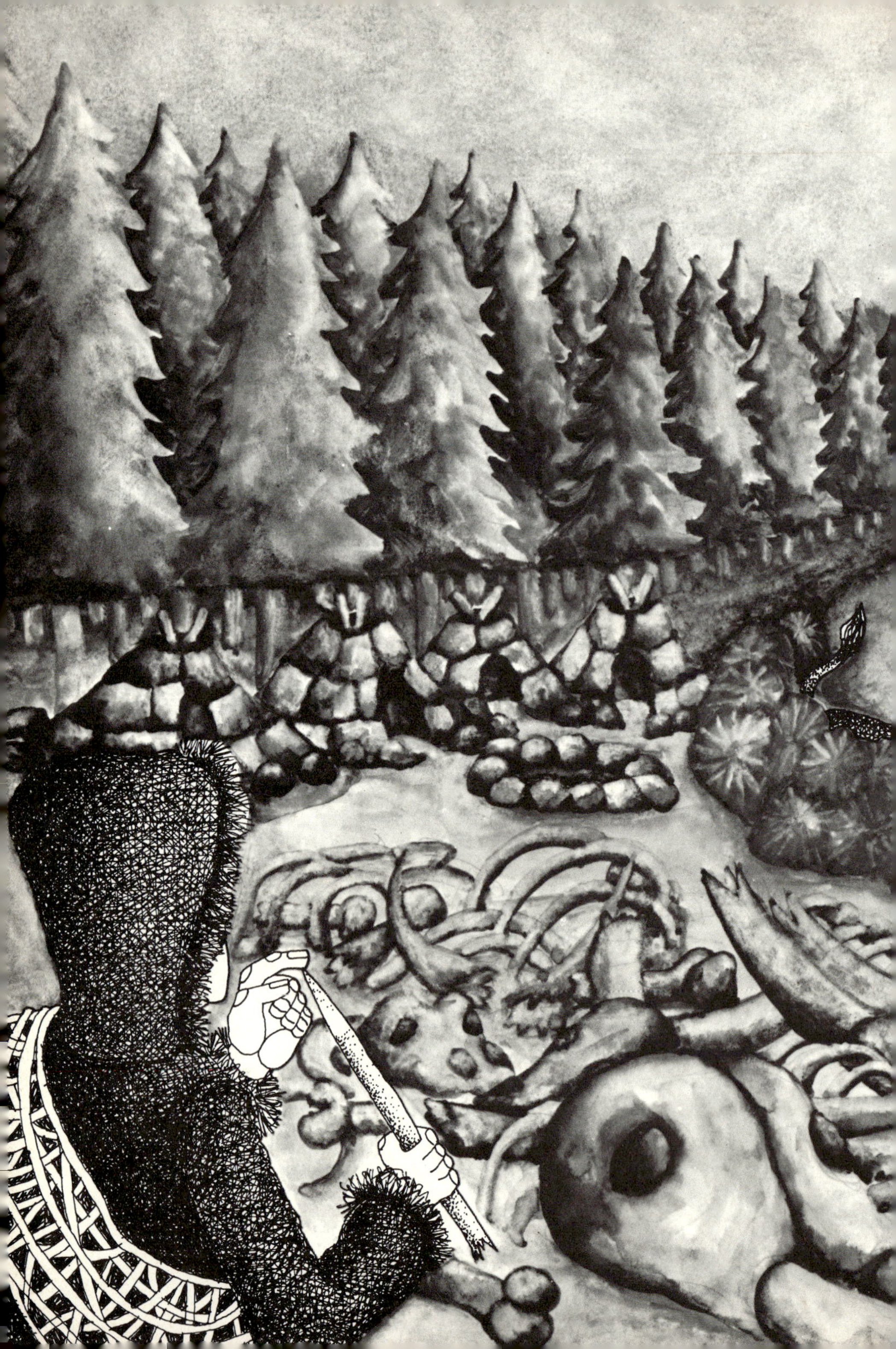

Homo Erectus

The Pleistocene – 750,000–300,000 years ago

A hunters' camp in a valley in Spain. But where are the hunters? Elephants, horses, deer, oxen, rhinos graze on the lush grass of the valley. The sound of the river fills the peaceful air.

Quizkid is dressed for a colder climate. He holds a wooden spear. But could it be used to kill an elephant?

The hunters' boneyard. They certainly did kill elephants, but how?

The hunters use fire to drive their prey into the swamps. The air is filled with the roar of flames and the trumpeting of the terrified animals.

The elephants make for the river, but are mired in the swamps and there meet their end. Quizkid is glad he is a primate with arms and hands to clutch and haul him to safety.

Homo Erectus

Eight hundred thousand years passed. Earth movements destroyed the lake at Olduvai where the australopithecines had lived, and buried their bones under layers of sediments. Another lake, another plain appeared, and another kind of fossil man lived there with the australopithecines. He is *Homo Erectus*.

He had no chin and no forehead, and massive brow ridges and jaws. Nevertheless his teeth and limbs were man-like, and his brain was twice the size of the australopithecine brain.

He lived among strange animals. There was a pig the size of a hippo, with tusks 1 metre (3 feet) long; a rhino twice as big as modern rhinos; a sheep bigger than a horse with a 1·8 metre (6 foot) horn span; a baboon the size of a gorilla, and a porcupine the size of a large dog. *Homo Erectus* had problems; he needed his bigger brain to help him survive, and he made himself new kinds of tools — hand axes, cleavers and picks.

Cleavers were like hand axes, but they had a straight cutting edge instead of a point. Picks were also like hand axes but bigger and heavier. The hand axe must have been a particularly useful tool because early men went on making them for half-a-million years.

Moving North

Sometime between 400,000 years and 700,000 years ago, early men of the *Homo Erectus* type began to wander north out of Africa and into Asia and Europe. Since man is an exploring animal there is, perhaps, no need to ask why these travellers left their homeland. The country lay open before them, and they went.

The last half of the Pleistocene was called the Great Ice Age. In fact there were four Ice Ages, as you can see from the chart, and between them were warmer 'interglacial periods'. These were the times when rhinos and hippos lived in the tropical pools and swamps of southern England.

The hand axe was not an axe at all, but a stone tool with one blunt and one pointed end and cutting edges along both sides.

years ago	division
	Holocene Epoch, begins c. 10,000 B.C.
80,000	Fourth, or Würm, Glacial Period
180,000	Third, or Last, Interglacial Period
220,000	Third, or Riss, Glacial Period
420,000	Second, or Great, Interglacial Period
460,000	Second, or Mindel, Glacial Period
560,000	First, or Early, Interglacial Period
620,000 or more	First, or Günz, Glacial Period

(Pleistocene Epoch or Great Ice Age)

Divisions of the Great Ice Age.

During the Ice Ages, glaciers, which are rivers of ice, moved south from the North Pole and shrouded large parts of the northern hemisphere in ice and snow.

Water from the sea turned into snow, which then fell on the land and was frozen. So the sea levels were lowered, and land bridges appeared.

The glaciers did not reach Africa, but the weather seems to have been cooler and wetter there during the glacial periods. The Sahara desert could be crossed, and *Homo Erectus* probably reached Europe, crossing through North Africa, Israel and Turkey. The islands of South East Asia were joined to the Asian continent, and some *Homo Erectus* bands turned east and wandered through India to China and Java.

Here they left their stones and bones. Thousands of years later Chinese apothecaries used 'dragon's teeth' ground into powder to make medicine. Then, in the 1920's, investigating palaeontologists discovered that the teeth were human, and they dug up fossils of *Homo Erectus*, about 64 kilometres (40 miles) south east of Peking.

Peking Man lived in China in the Middle Pleistocene. The fossils found belong to the Mindel-Riss Interglacial (see diagram on page 31) when the climate was warm and moist. His fellow mammals were the giant panda, the rhino, the elephant, the horse and the deer. These he hunted and cooked, and he left charred bones and blackened hearth-stones behind to prove it. He fought sabre-tooth tigers, and giant hyenas, and turned them out of their caves. He brought quartz crystals from some miles away and chipped them into tools, and he also made crude bone tools. Many of the skulls of Peking Man have sinister holes in them, made after death. Perhaps he was a cannibal. No tools have been found with the remains of *Java Man*, who was also *Homo Erectus*. He lived about 500,000 years ago.

In Europe *Homo Erectus* fossils have been found in Hungary and Spain and France.

There has been one mysterious discovery at Vallonet in south-eastern France. Here, in a cave overlooking the sea, pebble tools and the remains of rhinos, elephants, horses, and whales have been found. The fossils may be 750,000–1 million years old. But there are no hominid remains among them. Who chipped the tools and dragged the whale bones up from the beach? Could they have been adventurous australopithecines? Or did *Homo Erectus* arrive in Europe even earlier than had been thought? Somewhere the answers are buried in the earth.

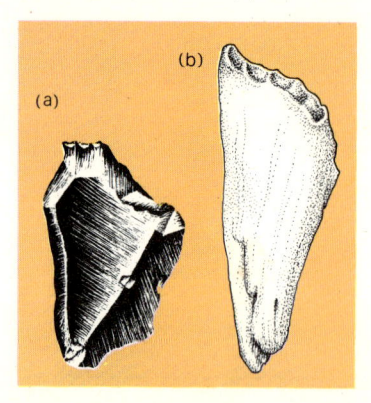

(a) A quartz crystal. (b) A broken animal bone. Tools made by Peking Man.

The Hunter's Brain

The really startling thing about *Homo Erectus* is the size of his brain.
In 2 million years his brain size nearly doubled. That is a very fast evolutionary change. What caused men with bigger brains to be so swiftly selected for survival?

Their hunting ability seems to provide the answer. A living floor at Torralba in Spain shows that *Homo Erectus* bands made a hunting camp there. One part of the camp was apparently used for killing and cutting up the game, another for cutting up the joints of meat, and a third for eating. The meat was scraped off the bones and then the bones were bashed to get at the marrow. The bones were those of

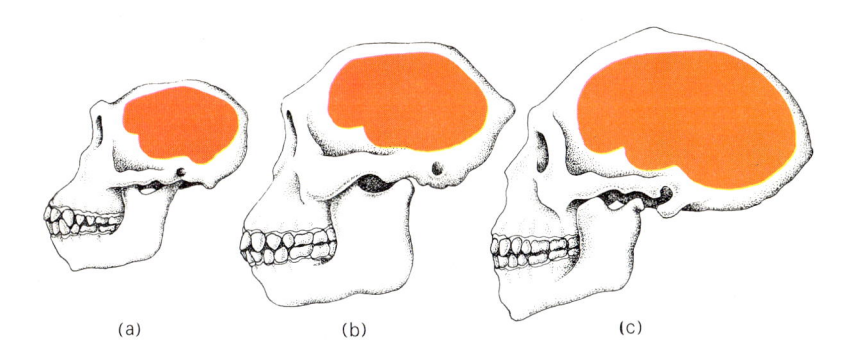

Brain sizes: (a) Chimpanzee. (b) Australopithecus. (c) Homo Erectus.

large, dangerous animals; elephants, rhinos and wild oxen. Patches of burned wood and carbon in the ancient valley seem to show that fires were used to drive game into the swamps.

For this kind of hunting you need men who can plan, men who can learn and remember, and men who can teach and pass on their knowledge. We shall never know what language they spoke, but they must have used one, for *Homo Erectus* children had a lot to learn.

To stay alive at all in the Ice-Age world needed resource and imagination. What Pleistocene genius thought of using nature's fire for his own purposes? Fire meant cooked food (and, perhaps, a longer life, because cooked food doesn't wear out the teeth so fast), comfort and warmth; longer days and safer nights, and a barrier between the hunters and the prowling carnivores.

Homo Erectus was drawing further away from the life of the animals who evolved along with him. He was re-shaping the world to suit himself.

Neanderthal Man

The Pleistocene — 75,000 years ago

In a cave in the mountains of Iraq lived people of the Neanderthal species.
One spring day, long ago, a man was killed by a falling rock and buried in the cave. His people picked wild flowers and lined the grave with them. Garlands of flowers were laid on top of it.

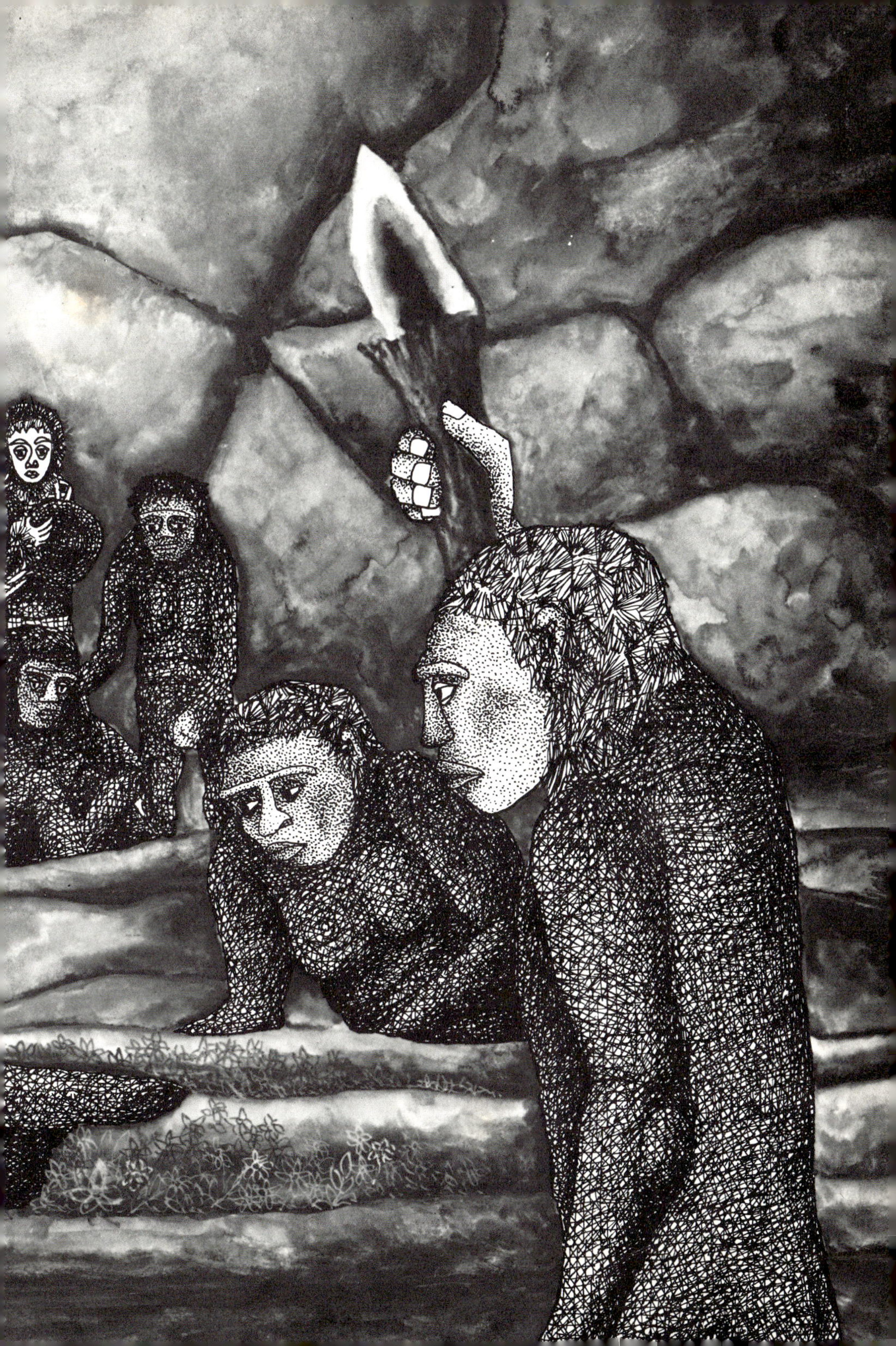

Neanderthal Man

Sometime during the next-to-last Ice Age in Europe, a new kind of man appeared. He was Neanderthal Man. His living floors have been found in Europe, Asia, Africa and the Middle East.

His appearance seems to have varied a good deal from place to place. Sometimes he looked like modern man, and sometimes he looked much more primitive. He was short and stocky, with powerful limbs and muscles. His brain was big, as big as that of modern man.

Neanderthal Man hunted the bison, the woolly mammoth, the woolly rhino, the wild horse and the fierce wild cattle of the Ice Age. He knew the hyena, the cave lion, and the leopard well.

He fought the cave bears for their homes and took possession of them.

He made dozens of different kinds of flint tools, hundreds and thousands of which have been found. Neanderthal men on their hunting grounds, and Neanderthal women at home in their caves and rock shelters, led busy lives. There were tools for killing, skinning, cutting, sawing, slicing, scraping, shredding, chopping, smoothing, boring, stripping and digging. Some of them seem to go together in 'toolkits', and it is possible to guess what kind of activities were going on in the different places.

Stone, and bone, and ivory tusks are what remain. Wood and plant fibres don't usually turn into fossils. But of course they used wood for posts, and tent poles, and what else? Racks for strips of meat, shredded and dried in the sun or over the fire, to eat in winter?

Early man looked around his world, at what Nature had provided for him, and he thought, imagined and invented.

Neanderthal Man buried his dead. This is something quite new in the history of man. Tools and food were placed in the graves.

He buried his dead and mourned them. In the Iraq cave, the people lined the grave with flowers — the ancestors of grape hyacinths, daisies, groundsel and mallow. Flowers were woven into branches, to make a wreath. (We know because the fossil pollen has been found.)

Neanderthal Man was powerfully built and a skilled hunter; he had fire and tools, and there were plenty of animals. He tackled danger bravely. Yet he vanished about 35,000 years ago. Why?

He was adapted to the blizzards and snow drifts and knifing winds of the Ice Age. He probably lived in small isolated groups. Perhaps he

These are Neanderthal tools. What do you think they might have been used for?

Neanderthal tool kit.

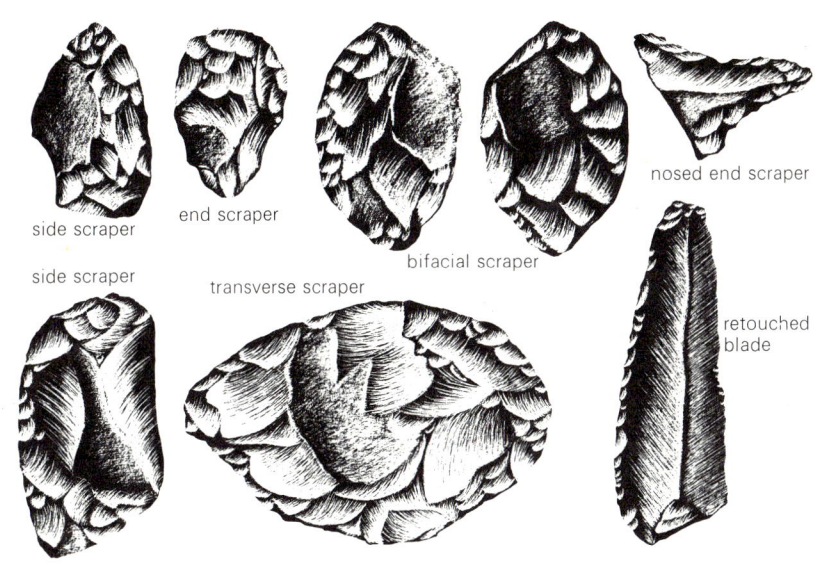

side scraper
end scraper
bifacial scraper
nosed end scraper
side scraper
transverse scraper
retouched blade

could not adapt to the better weather. Perhaps the small groups grew smaller, and simply died out. Or, perhaps, in other places in the world, he met and bred with *Homo sapiens*, modern man.

Perhaps we have inherited some of his genes.

Homo Sapiens

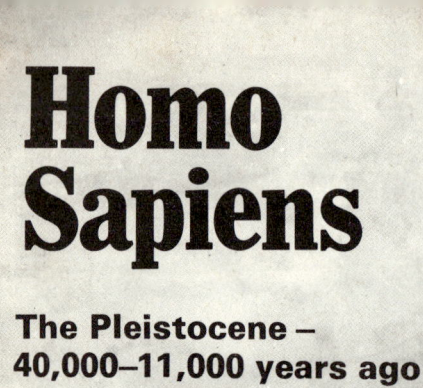

The Pleistocene – 40,000–11,000 years ago

A quiet autumn morning in a Magdalenian home 11,000 years ago. The hunters are away.

The people of the Upper Stone Age made clothes of skin, sewn with bone needles. They probably used sinews for thread.

Is he a trader? He has treasures to show. The flint blade is an 'antique', made 4,000 years before.

Quizkid would like to explore the cave.

Hunters wore antlers to stalk their prey and they had 'machines' — spear-throwers, to make the spear go farther.

The little girl shows the man a treasure of her own. It is far more ancient than either of them know.

Round stones were heated and dropped into a leather container of water to boil it for cooking.

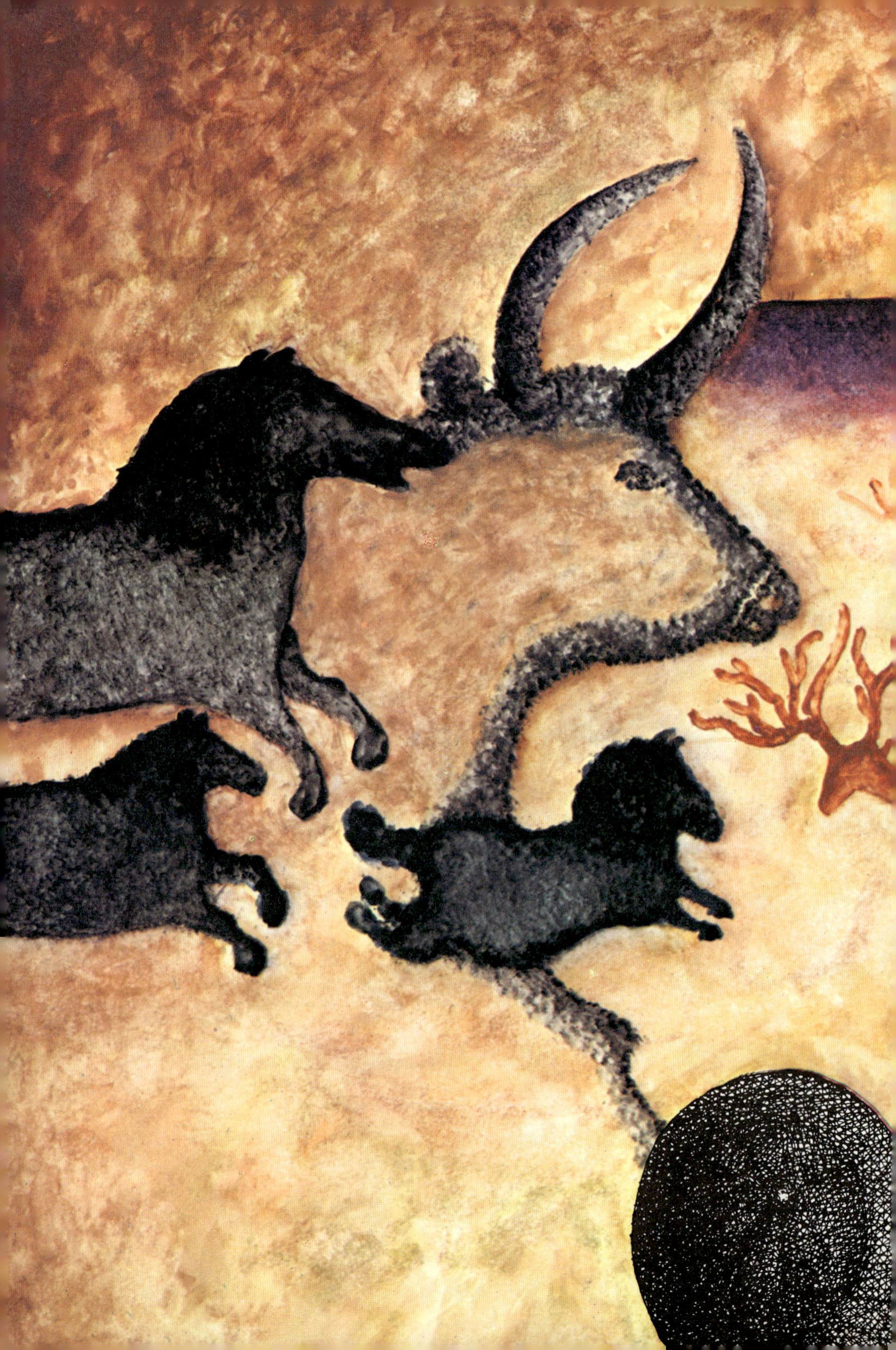

The flickering light from the stone lamp makes the painted animals seem alive. Did the hunters come here to dance, to pray, to make powerful magic for their dangerous work?

Homo Sapiens

Sometime between 30,000 and 40,000 years ago human hunters of a different species appeared in Europe. They had domed heads and high foreheads, and brow ridges that were hardly noticeable; their faces were pulled back under the smooth brow and forehead. This was *Homo sapiens*, 'Man the Wise', the only kind of man living in the world today.

Nobody knows where *Homo sapiens* came from. Some very early remains in England (Swanscombe Man), and in Germany and Hungary and China and South Africa suggest that *Homo sapiens* men were alive while *Homo neanderthalensis* and even *Homo erectus* were still around.

But wherever he came from, we know him best from the record he left in France during the last half of the last glacial period, the Würm.

The period in which these new hunters lived in Europe is called the Upper Palaeolithic (Pal-eeo-LITH-ic), or Late Stone Age. There seem to have been four main groups, each making different kinds of tools. They are:

1. The *Perigordian* (Perry-GOR-deean) people. They lived from 35,000 to 22,000 years ago, and in their tool kits is found a special kind of flint knife.

Skull of Homo sapiens.

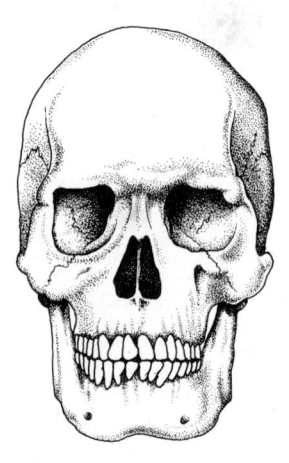

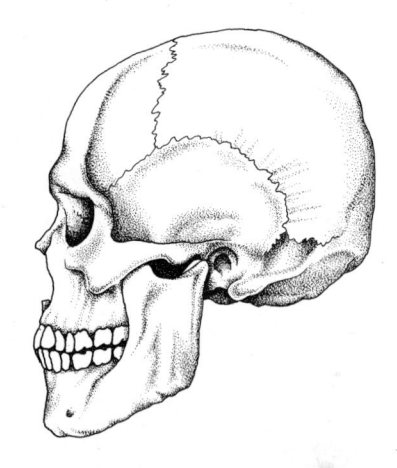

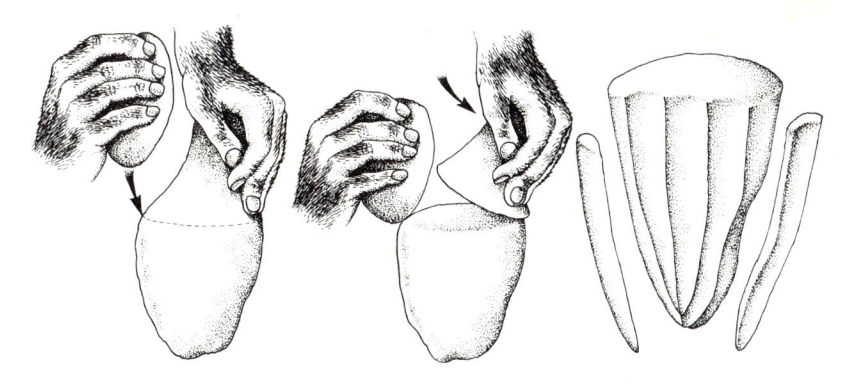

Making a punched blade tool.

To make a blade like this you take a lump of flint, rest a pointed piece of bone on top, near the edge, and hit the bone. This chips off a narrow flake, which can be further shaped into a knife. Skilful craftsmen could probably turn them out fast whenever they were needed.

2. The *Aurignacian* (Aw-ri-NAY-see-an) people lived at the same time as the Perigordians. They made tools like those below right:

Aurignacian tools were heavier, and the knives, scrapers and chisels were wider. They also made bone spear heads, split at the base so that they could be fitted onto wooden shafts.

3. The *Solutrean* (So-LOU-tree-an) people lived from 20,000 to 17,000 years ago in mountainous country in south east France, at a time when the weather was particularly severe. Nevertheless their craftsmen kept warm enough to make particularly beautiful tools in what are called the 'laurel leaf' and 'willow leaf' patterns. These blades

Typical Perigordian blade.

Typical Aurignacian tools.

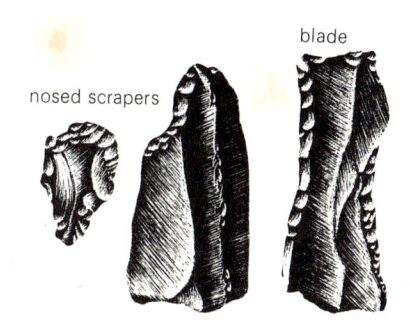

nosed scrapers   blade

(a) Solutrean arrow head.
(b) Solutrean 'laurel leaf' blade.

were fragile and most delicately chipped.

Some of these blades were far too delicate to use. They would have snapped. This is the first time we find man making objects that were beautiful but apparently useless. Perhaps they did have a use, but what was it?

The Solutrean people probably used bows and arrows; and a few bone needles have been found.

4. The *Magdalenians* (Mag-da-LANE-eeans). They were powerful reindeer hunters, and there were many of them. Perhaps 50,000 people lived in France from 17,000 to 12,000 years ago.

In Magdalenian times the environment changed. The glaciers began to retreat, the sea levels rose, the rushing rivers were full of fish, and in the spring the air was full of migrating birds on their way to their breeding grounds. People seem to have lived in year-round settlements.

The Magdalenians made tools of bone and antler and ivory, and often they decorated them. They made two new kinds of tool, the harpoon and the spear-thrower.

The spear-thrower makes the spear go faster and farther than ordinary muscle power can send it.

Bone needles are plentiful in Magdalenian remains, so these people had skin clothes made to fit them.

But above all, the Magdalenians were artists.

Aurignacian men had scratched the outlines of animals on cave walls. Magdalenian men painted their walls. In sixty-five places in France, and thirty in Spain — and probably in other places as yet undiscovered — we have found beautiful paintings of antlered deer, strong little horses, and powerful bulls.

There are hardly any drawings of people, and no flowers, or trees, or waterfalls. We wish they had drawn people, but instead we must be content with looking at animals that no one has seen alive since the last Ice Age.

For paint the artists used various coloured earths; they ground them to powder and mixed them with fat.

Mysteriously, many of the most beautiful paintings are found far back in caves, sometimes in corners and crevices where they are hard to see. For light to paint by, the artists used stone lamps with moss wicks.

We shall probably never know what the cave paintings meant to the men of the Late Stone Age. What rituals and ceremonies took place? Were the paintings made for hunting magic? Did the hunters believe that the animal made to appear on the wall would appear on the hunting ground and become their victim? Or were the paintings backgrounds, stage sets for their dramas based on hunting? Bone whistles and pipes have been found in some of the caves. Did the hunters dance to music? Were there drums too?

All we know is that these beautiful, swift, strong animals must always have been in their minds and their dreams.

Perhaps, in a way they did not realize, the Palaeolithic artists were saying farewell to the animal world and their splendid hunting days. Time and change, which make everything in the world, were soon to bring quite new ways of living for modern man.

(a) Magdalenian harpoons.
(b) A Magdalenian spear-thrower, carved with a horse and a deer.

Time and Change

The earth is at least 4,600 million years old.

Man's development, from a tiny tree-dwelling primate to *Homo sapiens*, seems infinitely slow, yet on the calendar of geological time it is extremely fast. It is only a very few million years since the australopithecines shivered in the African night and hunted small game by day.

Imagine a tree growing at the rate of 2mm (about $\frac{1}{16}$th of an inch) every thousand years, planted 600 million years ago. This would be in Cambrian times (the first faint traces of life begin to appear in Cambrian rocks). The tree would now be more than a mile high.

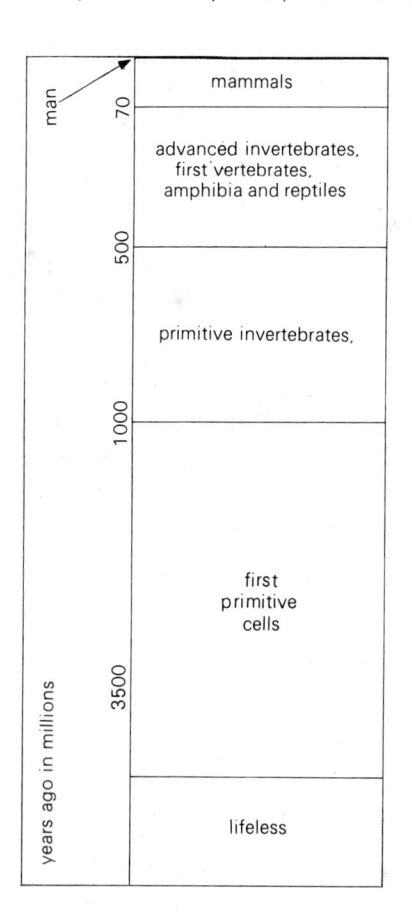

Imagine a film, lasting a year, and beginning on 1 January with the origin of the earth. The Lower Cambrian would begin on 18 November, and man would appear about twenty minutes to midnight on 31 December. So old is the earth, and so new is man.

Since the first hominid used the first tool, there have been two kinds of evolution. One is the slow process of Natural Selection. The other is a different kind: man's children inherit not only genes, but knowledge. Man adapts the environment to suit himself. He doesn't wait for change; he makes it.

Ten million years from now, what will the palaeontologists of the future find?

years ago in millions	
man — 70	mammals
500	advanced invertebrates, first vertebrates, amphibia and reptiles
1000	primitive invertebrates,
3500	first primitive cells
	lifeless

Time and Change: The Development of Life on Earth.

Time Chart

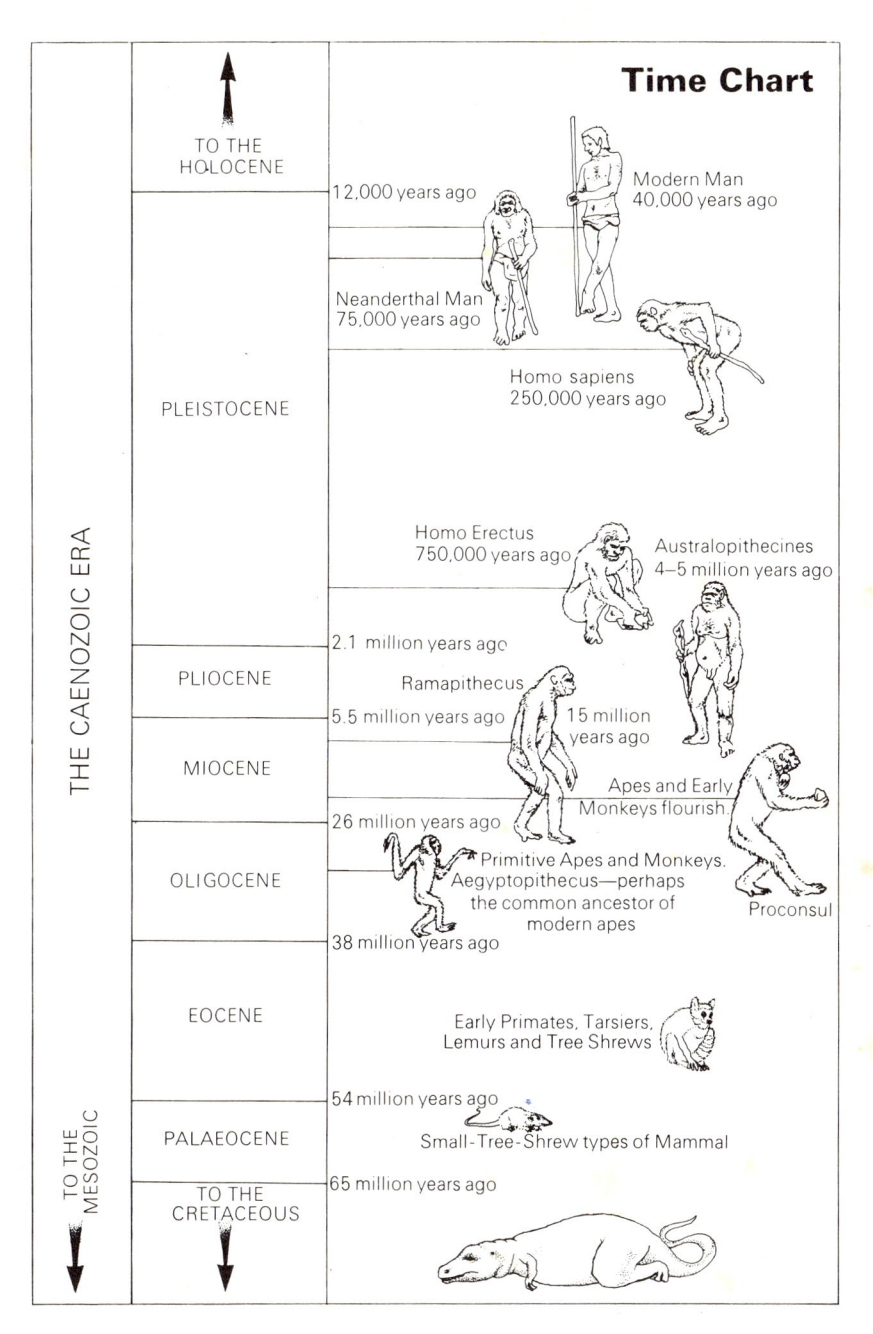

THE CAENOZOIC ERA

↑ TO THE HOLOCENE

PLEISTOCENE
- 12,000 years ago
- Modern Man 40,000 years ago
- Neanderthal Man 75,000 years ago
- Homo sapiens 250,000 years ago
- Homo Erectus 750,000 years ago
- Australopithecines 4–5 million years ago

PLIOCENE
- 2.1 million years ago
- Ramapithecus 15 million years ago
- 5.5 million years ago

MIOCENE
- Apes and Early Monkeys flourish
- 26 million years ago

OLIGOCENE
- Primitive Apes and Monkeys. Aegyptopithecus—perhaps the common ancestor of modern apes
- Proconsul
- 38 million years ago

EOCENE
- Early Primates, Tarsiers, Lemurs and Tree Shrews
- 54 million years ago

PALAEOCENE
- Small-Tree-Shrew types of Mammal
- 65 million years ago

↕ TO THE MESOZOIC / TO THE CRETACEOUS

47

Index

Adapis, 6
Aegyptopithecus, 16, 47
Africa, 16, 19, 24, 30, 31, 42
Anthropoidea, 17-18
Arrowhead, Solutrean, 44
Aurignacians, 43, 44
Australopithecines, 19-25, 30, 32, 33, 46, 47
Australopithecus africanus, 24
  robustus, 24

Baboon, 'threat' face, 18.
Birds, related to dinosaurs, 5
Boiling stones, 39
Bone tools, 17, 22, 32, 43, 44
  whistles, 45
Brain sizes, comparative, 9, 10, 24, 30, 32-3, 36
Burials, Neanderthal, 34-6

Caenozoic Era, 47
Cambrian, The, 46
Canine teeth, 8, 17, 24
Cave bear, 36
Cave paintings, 40-41, 44-5
Ceboidea, 18
Cercopithecoidea, 18
China, 31, 32, 42
Chordata, 9
Classification of animals, 9
  of primates, 9, 17-18
Cleavers, stone, 30
Coryphodon, 7

Development of life on earth, 46-7
Diatryma, 6
Dinosaurs, 3, 5, 8

East Rudolph, Kenya, 25
Egypt, 16
England, 30, 42
Eocene, The, 4-11, 16, 47
Eohippus, 6
Ethiopia, 24
Evolution, how it works, 11
Eyes, development of, in early primates, 9, 10

Fire, 22, 28, 33, 36
Flint tools, 36, 39, 42-4
Flowers, in Neanderthal burial, 34, 36
France, 32, 42, 43, 44

Genes, 11, 37, 46
Germany, 42
Giant hogs, 14

Glaciers, 31, 44
Grave, Neanderthal, 34-6
Great Ice Age, 30-31, 33
Günz, Ice Age, 31

Hands, importance of, 9
Hand axe, 30
Harpoon, Magdalenian, 44, 45
Hominidae, 17, 18
Hominoidea, 18
Homo erectus, 30-33, 42, 47
  habilis, 25
  neanderthalensis, 34-7, 42, 47
  sapiens, 37, 38-45, 46, 47
Hungary, 32, 42
Hunting, importance of, in evolution, 32-3
Hyaenodon, 6

Ice Ages (chart), 31
India, 16, 31
Interglacials, 30-31
Iraq, 34, 36
Israel, 31

Java Man, 32
Jaws, australopithecine, compared with ape, 24

Kenyapithecus, 16
Kingdom, animal, 9

Lamps, Stone Age, 41, 45
Late Stone Age, 42-5
'Laurel leaf' tools, 43-4
Lemur, 9, 17, 47
Libytherium, 25
Living floor, 25

Magdalenians, 38-41, 44-5
Mammalian Design, 8
Mindel-Riss Interglacial, 31, 32
Miocene, The, 14-18, 24, 47
Miocene monkeys, 14
Mutations, 11

Natural Selection, 11, 46
Neanderthal Man, 34-7, 42, 47

Olduvai Gorge, Tanzania, 25, 30
Oligocene, The, 16, 47

Palaeocene, The, 47
Pebble tools, 23, 25, 32
Peking Man, 32
Perigordians, 42-3
Picks, stone, 30
Pleistocene, The, 24, 27-45, 47

Pliocene, The, 24, 47
Pollen, fossil, 36
Pongidae, 18
Primates, early, 4-11
  classification of, 9, 17-18
Proconsul, 16, 47
Prosimii, 17
Punched blade tools, 43

Quizkid prepares for his journey, 3
  afloat on Eocene seas, 4-5
  in an Eocene forest, 6-7
  with a *Ramapithecus* family, 12-13
  with the australopithecines, 19-23
  at a *Homo Erectus* camp, 26-9
  at a Neanderthal funeral, 34-5
  in a Magdalenian home, 38-9
  in the painted caves, 40-41

Ramapithecus, 12-18, 47
Riss Ice Age, 31

Skull, of *Homo sapiens*, 42
Snake, Eocene, 7
Solutreans, 43-4
'Southern Apes', 24
Spain, 27, 32, 44
Spear-thrower, 39, 44, 45
Stereoscopic vision, 9
Swanscombe Man, 42

Tarsioid, 6, 10, 16
Teeth, mammalian, 8, 17, 24
Time and Change, 45, 46-7
Time Chart, 47
Tree dwellers, 6, 8-11, 17, 46
Tree Shrew, Eocene, 4, 9, 10, 47
Tools:
  Aurignacian, 43
  Australopithecine, 23-4, 25
  Magdalenian, 44-5
  Neanderthal, 36-7
  Peking Man, 32
  Perigordian, 42-3
  Solutrean, 43-4
Torralba, 32

Uintatherium, 7
Upper Stone Age, 38-45

Vallonet, prehistoric site at, 32

Whale, Eocene, 4
'Willow leaf' tools, 43
Würm, Ice Age, 31, 42

48